Look Who's Outdoors
Adventure Challenge
"Everything Outdoors"

By
Khamra Echols

Khamra Echols

Copyright © 2024

Dedication

To all those who embrace the call of the wild, whose spirits are stirred by the beauty of nature, and whose hearts beat to the rhythm of adventure. May this book inspire you to explore, to discover, and to forge unforgettable connections in the great outdoors.

Table of Contents

Dedication iii
Chapter 1 Setting the Stage for Adventure 6
Chapter 2 Let the Adventure Begin 11
Chapter 3 Connecting with Nature 17
Chapter 4 Embracing the Adventure Ahead 23
    Anticipating the Journey Together: 23
    Packing Essentials and Collaborating: 24
    Building Group Cohesion: 26
    A Reflection 26
Chapter 5 Week 1 - Cycling Harmony 29
    The Thrill of Two Wheels 29
    Gear Up for Adventure 30
    Exploring New Horizons 32
    Challenges and Triumphs 32
    Embracing the Journey 32
    Justin Deshone: The Student's Champion 33
Chapter 6 Week 2 – Waterside Adventures 35
    Introduction to Water Adventures 35
    Preparing for Aquatic Excursions 37
    Challenges and Triumphs 38
    Embracing Group Bonding Moments 39
    Chevaughn Dixon: Paddling Towards Equity and Adventure 39
Chapter 7 Week 3 – Climbing Together 42
    Understanding Group Climbing 42

Choosing Your Climbing Challenge...42

Supporting Each Other...43

Gaining New Perspectives 44

Personal Anecdotes..46

Chapter 8 Week 4 - Thrill Seekers Unite 48

Preparing for Extreme Experiences 48

Encouraging Each Other's Courage...50

Treasuring Shared Moments of Thrill..50

Personal Reflections...51

Chapter 9 Reflecting on the Journey Together 53

Celebrating Group Growth and Connections...................................53

Expressing Gratitude and Appreciation 54

Setting Intentions for Future Adventures...55

Expressing Love and Commitment..56

Personal Reflections...56

Chapter 10 Continuing the Adventure Together.................................59

Looking Ahead to New Adventures 59

Setting Group Goals...60

Final Thoughts and Farewell 61

Personal Reflections...62

Chapter 1
Setting the Stage for Adventure

Welcome, adventurers! Join me in the great outdoors, where excitement fills the air and every path leads to fresh revelations. I'm Khamra Echols, here to lead you through the endless realm of outdoor exploration. I'm excited to take you on an adventure that will awaken your senses, push your boundaries, and shape your experiences like never before.

Picture yourself standing on the brink of a new day, the freshness of dawn enveloping you like a comforting embrace. The morning breeze dances lightly against your skin, sending shivers of anticipation down your spine. Inhale deeply, and you're greeted by the earthy perfume of pine needles mingled with the rich scent of damp soil, a fragrance that speaks of life and renewal.

As the sun begins its ascent, its gentle rays filter through the dense canopy above, creating a mesmerizing play of light and shadow on the forest floor. Shafts of sunlight pierce through the leaves, illuminating patches of vibrant greenery and casting a golden glow on the trail ahead. Each step forward feels like a promise of discovery, an invitation to unravel the mysteries hidden within the wilderness.

The tranquility of the moment is palpable, filling you with a sense of serenity and awe. Nature's symphony surrounds you – the chirping of birds, the rustle of leaves, the distant babble of a nearby stream – all blending harmoniously into a melody of life. It's a scene so breathtakingly beautiful that it stirs something deep within your soul, igniting a longing for adventure and exploration.

In this fleeting moment, you're reminded of the boundless magic that awaits in the great outdoors – a world where every sight, sound, and scent has the power to awaken your senses and stir your spirit. It's a reminder that amidst the chaos of daily life, there's solace to be found in the simplicity of nature and that sometimes, the greatest adventures begin with a single step into the unknown.

Look Who's Outdoor

Our journey isn't just about wandering through the wilderness; it's a profound expedition into the depths of our own beings. As we traverse the rugged terrain, our muscles ache, and our hearts race with the anticipation of what lies ahead. Yet, with each step forward, we delve deeper into the essence of who we are.

Amidst the towering trees and jagged rocks, we confront obstacles that test our resolve and push us to our limits. There are moments when doubt creeps in, when fear whispers in our ears, urging us to retreat. But we press on, fueled by a flickering ember of determination that refuses to be extinguished.

In the face of adversity, we discover reservoirs of strength we never knew existed – a primal force that surges through our veins, propelling us forward with unwavering resolve. With every obstacle conquered, we feel a sense of empowerment wash over us, like a beacon of light cutting through the darkness.

But it's not just physical strength that we unearth on this journey; it's the resilience of the human spirit. We learn to embrace discomfort, to dance with uncertainty, and to find beauty in the midst of chaos. Each challenge becomes an opportunity for growth, a chance to shed our old selves and emerge transformed, like a phoenix rising from the ashes.

And in our moments of triumph, we don't just celebrate individual victories; we celebrate the collective triumph of humanity. We are reminded that we are not alone on this journey and that our shared struggles and our shared triumphs bind us together. As we stand atop the mountain peak, gazing out at the vast expanse before us, we are filled with a profound sense of gratitude – for the journey, the challenges, and the opportunity to discover the depths of our own humanity.

In the heart of outdoor adventure lies a profound opportunity to weave intricate webs of connection between individuals. Amidst the soaring peaks and rushing rivers, the true essence of human connection reveals itself – raw, unfiltered, and utterly transformative.

Imagine standing shoulder to shoulder with fellow adventurers poised at the foot of a formidable mountain or the edge of a rushing river. In those moments, a palpable sense of anticipation hangs in the air, mingling with the shared excitement and trepidation that courses through every fiber of your being.

As you embark on the journey together, navigating the twists and turns of the terrain or the ebbs and flows of the river, a silent understanding begins to form between you. It's a silent pact, forged in the crucible of adventure, that binds you together in a bond stronger than any words could convey.

In the face of adversity, you find yourselves leaning on each other for support, drawing strength from the collective determination that propels you forward. Each obstacle becomes an opportunity to strengthen your connection as you work together to overcome challenges that seem insurmountable on your own.

But it's not just the shared triumphs that deepen the bonds between you; it's the shared vulnerabilities as well. In moments of exhaustion or uncertainty, you find solace in the knowledge that you're not alone – that there are others who understand your struggles and are there to lift you up when you falter.

And as you reach the summit of the mountain or paddle across the final stretch of the river, the sense of camaraderie that fills the air is almost tangible. It's a feeling of accomplishment, of shared victory, but more than that; it's a recognition of the profound connections that have been forged along the way – connections that will endure long after the adventure has ended.

Ultimately, these connections – born from shared experiences, fueled by mutual respect, and nurtured by a sense of belonging – make outdoor adventure such a powerful and transformative journey. For in the wilderness, amidst the vastness of nature's embrace, we discover not only the beauty of the world around us but also the beauty of the human spirit, united in a common quest for exploration, growth, and connection.

But let's not tarry any longer – it's time to plunge into the heart of our adventure. Throughout this book, we'll embark on an array of outdoor escapades, each promising to ignite your senses and quicken your pulse. Get ready for a journey through landscapes that will leave you breathless and moments that will etch themselves into your memory.

Imagine trekking through dense jungles, where each step is a dance with nature's untamed beauty. The air hums with the chorus of exotic creatures, their calls mingling with the rustle of leaves and the soft patter of raindrops. Every footfall brings you deeper into this lush wilderness, where ancient trees stand sentinel and hidden wonders await discovery.

Or picture standing at the base of a towering mountain, its snow-capped peak reaching toward the sky. As you begin your ascent, the air grows thinner, your muscles straining with each step. Yet, with every labored breath, you feel a sense of exhilaration building within you, driving you toward the summit. And when you finally reach the top, the world unfolds in a breathtaking panorama – a testament to the power of perseverance and the beauty of nature.

But our adventures won't end there. We'll dive into crystal-clear waters, exploring vibrant coral reefs and mysterious underwater caves. We'll navigate rushing rivers and rugged canyons, feeling the rush of adrenaline as we conquer whitewater rapids and scale sheer cliffs.

With each turn of the page, you'll find yourself swept up in a whirlwind of emotions – the thrill of discovery, the awe of witnessing nature's grandeur, and the profound sense of connection that comes from immersing yourself in the great outdoors. So buckle up, for the journey of a lifetime awaits.

What truly makes this journey special are the stories – the real, honest tales of people whose lives have been changed by their adventures outdoors. We'll meet folks from all walks of life – some who've been exploring for years and others who are just starting out.

Through their stories, we'll learn how outdoor adventures can change us in big ways.

Get ready to hear stories of success and struggle, of thrilling highs and deep thoughts. We'll hear from adventurers who've faced danger and come out stronger and from others who've found peace and healing in nature. Each story will teach us something about ourselves and the world around us.

So, are you ready to join me on this journey? Are you prepared to step out of your comfort zone and discover what you're truly capable of? If you are, then grab your gear, and let's go explore. The wilderness is calling – let's answer it together!

Chapter 2
Let the Adventure Begin

In the lush forests of Georgia, where tall pine trees sway gently in the breeze, Offgrid Kid's adventure unfolds with each new day. His story is full of perseverance, teamwork, and a deep love for nature, showing us the importance of being prepared and exploring together.

Every morning brings a fresh start for Offgrid Kid as he explores the wilderness, surrounded by friends who share his passion. Through his journey, we learn that being ready and working together can make a big difference, creating unforgettable experiences and lasting bonds.

In Georgia's wild beauty, where nature's secrets whisper and the landscape stretches endlessly, Offgrid Kid's expedition is a reminder of the joy and growth found in exploring the great outdoors with friends.

As dawn paints the horizon with its palette of gold and crimson hues, Offgrid Kid stands poised on the threshold of another day ripe with possibility. Yet, for him, adventure transcends mere physical exploration; it embodies a mindset steeped in resilience and optimism, propelling him ever forward on his journey.

From the tender age of six, Offgrid Kid has imbibed his father's wisdom like a revitalizing tonic, recognizing that each trial encountered catalyzes personal growth. His father's tales of overcoming adversity, woven with threads of unwavering determination and resilient hope, have left an indelible mark upon Offgrid Kid's impressionable heart.

"I can still vividly recall my first foray into the woods," Offgrid Kid reminisces, a nostalgic smile playing upon his lips. "Fear undoubtedly gripped me. Yet, guided by my father's words of wisdom, I came to understand that every setback is but an opportunity in disguise. And so, I summoned my courage, relied on my instincts, and eventually found my way home. That pivotal moment taught me a profound lesson—that adventure isn't about avoiding obstacles; it's about confronting them head-on."

As the morning light bathes the world in its gentle embrace, Offgrid Kid carries with him the enduring lessons gleaned from his father's guidance. Armed with a spirit fortified by resilience and optimism, he strides forth into the unknown, ready to embrace the challenges that lie ahead as opportunities for growth and discovery. For Offgrid Kid, each obstacle encountered is not a barrier to be circumvented but a stepping stone on the path to personal transformation and self-realization.

Through the lens of Offgrid Kid's experiences, readers are transported into a world where resilience isn't simply a trait but an essential guiding principle. From navigating dense forests to weathering storms—both literal and metaphorical—Offgrid Kid and his family epitomize the strength derived from maintaining a positive perspective in the face of adversity.

Preparing for adventure extends far beyond the practicalities of packing supplies and charting routes; it entails the meticulous cultivation of both physical prowess and mental resilience, serving as the bedrock of their exploration.

In the ethereal glow of dawn, before the sun bathes the landscape in its warm embrace, Offgrid Kid and his family assemble for their daily ritual of physical conditioning and mental fortitude. With muscles primed and minds honed to a keen edge, they embark on a journey of self-discovery that transcends the mere physical realm.

As the first light of day filters through the verdant canopy above, casting dappled shadows on the forest floor, Offgrid Kid and his companions embrace the challenges that lie ahead with unwavering determination. With each step, each breath, they delve deeper into the vast expanse of their potential, pushing the boundaries of what they once deemed possible.

In this sacred hour, amidst the tranquil beauty of the natural world, they forge bonds that are as resilient as the very earth beneath their feet. Through shared exertion and mutual support, they strengthen not only their bodies but also their spirits, united in their pursuit of the unknown and the endless possibilities that await on the horizon.

"We kick off each morning with a routine of exercises aimed at boosting our strength, flexibility, and stamina," Offgrid Kid explains, his eyes gleaming with youthful excitement. "Whether it's jogging along trails or scaling trees, we push ourselves to the max, knowing that every drop of sweat brings us closer to our objectives."

In the soft light of dawn, amidst the rustling leaves and the crisp morning air, Offgrid Kid and his companions embark on their physical regimen. With each step, each stretch, they fuel their bodies with determination, embracing the challenge of honing their physical prowess to its peak.

Yet, physical readiness is just one side of the coin. During the serene moments of quiet reflection that follow, Offgrid Kid and his kin delve into the depths of their minds, sharpening their focus and steeling their resolve for the hurdles ahead.

"Mindfulness is crucial," Offgrid Kid's father affirms, his voice a steady anchor amidst the swirling doubts. "In the heat of the moment, when adrenaline surges like wildfire, it's easy to lose sight of our aims. But by centering ourselves, by directing our energy with pinpoint accuracy, we can accomplish feats we never deemed possible."

In the tranquil embrace of nature, surrounded by the whispering trees and the gentle babble of nearby streams, they cultivate a sense of inner balance, harnessing the power of their minds as keenly as they do their bodies. It is through this harmonious union of physical prowess and mental fortitude that they forge ahead, ready to conquer whatever challenges lie in their path.

Truly, Offgrid Kid's journey stands as a testament to the profound impact of readiness—both physical and mental—on the pursuit of adventure. Day by day, he hones his skills, bolsters his resolve, and emerges from trials stronger, wiser, and more resilient than before.

However, Offgrid Kid is eager to emphasize that adventure isn't merely a solitary endeavor but rather a joint voyage that weaves together hearts and minds in a tapestry of trust, communication, and mutual encouragement.

Beneath the tranquil shade of the forest canopy, where sunlight filters through the leaves like scattered jewels, Offgrid Kid and his family gather to strengthen the bonds that unite them. Amidst the rustling leaves and the gentle murmur of the breeze, they come together, sharing stories, laughter, and dreams. Through shared escapades and collective victories, they cultivate a camaraderie that transcends the bounds of mere familial relations.

In these moments of shared joy and camaraderie, amidst the serenity of the natural world, Offgrid Kid and his loved ones find solace and strength, drawing inspiration from one another as they continue their journey into the unknown. For them, adventure isn't just about individual achievement but about the shared experiences that forge unbreakable bonds and memories that will last a lifetime.

"Trust is the cornerstone of any successful adventure," Offgrid Kid's mother affirms, her voice a gentle echo in the vast expanse of the wilderness. "When you're out in the wild, miles away from civilization, you have no choice but to rely on each other. And that trust, that unspoken bond between kindred spirits, is what gives us the courage to press on, even when the path ahead is shrouded in darkness."

In Offgrid Kid's world, communication is not merely a means to an end but a lifeline that connects hearts across the vast expanse of the wilderness. Through whispered words and knowing glances, he and his family navigate the treacherous terrain of the unknown, each step guided by the collective wisdom of the group.

"We listen to each other," Offgrid Kid explains, his voice tinged with reverence for the lessons learned amidst the silence of the forest. "We respect each other's opinions, even when they differ from our own. And through open dialogue and honest communication, we chart a course that leads us ever closer to our shared goals."

As the day draws to a close and the last vestiges of sunlight fade into the embrace of twilight, Offgrid Kid invites readers to embark on a journey of self-discovery that mirrors his own. Through prompts for personal reflection and introspection, he encourages them to ponder their readiness for adventure – both in the wilderness and in the vast expanse of their own lives.

"Adventure begins within," Offgrid Kid asserts, his voice a gentle reminder of the untapped potential that lies dormant within each of us. "It's not just about climbing mountains or traversing deserts; it's about embracing the unknown with an open heart and an open mind. And by taking the time to reflect on our fears, our aspirations, and our deepest desires, we can unlock the door to a world of endless possibility."

In the quiet solitude of journaling, readers find solace amidst the chaos of everyday life, their thoughts flowing like a river through the fertile landscape of their minds. Through the act of introspection, they uncover hidden truths and untapped reservoirs of strength that serve as the foundation for their adventures yet to come.

In the heart of the Georgia backwoods, a place where nature holds sway and the symphony of the forest dances in harmony, the tale of Offgrid Kid unfolds with all the enchantment of a story woven from the very fabric of imagination itself. Through the steadfast resolve of a young adventurer, meticulous planning, and the unyielding support of family ties, they carve a trail through the untamed wilderness, a journey that not only stretches to the distant horizons but delves into the profound depths of the human spirit.

Under the celestial canopy, where stars glitter like celestial diamonds strewn across the velvet expanse of the night sky, Offgrid Kid's voice rings out, a clarion call echoing through the tranquil stillness. "Adventure awaits," his whispered words carry, a vow of boundless excitement and endless opportunity. "With courage as your compass and curiosity as your guide, the possibilities are limitless."

As you absorb the stirring resonance of Offgrid Kid's words, do you sense that stirring within your soul? Have you come to realize that the essence of the journey lies not solely in reaching a predefined destination, but in the profound embrace of the voyage itself? With each syllable lingering in the recesses of your mind, can you feel the surge of anticipation, urging you to venture forth into the vast expanse of the unknown?

Chapter 3
Connecting with Nature

As the sun begins its slow descent beyond the horizon, casting a golden hue over the tranquil landscape, we find ourselves drawn to the call of nature. In this chapter, we embark on a journey of self-discovery and connection, exploring the profound impact that our relationship with the natural world holds. From childhood memories to transformative outdoor experiences, we delve deep into the heart of human-nature connections, seeking to understand the intrinsic bond that unites us with the wilderness.

Close your eyes for a moment and let your mind drift back to the days of your childhood. Can you vividly recall the first time you felt the cool, dew-drenched grass beneath your bare feet? Or the exhilarating rush of wind as you soar high on a swing, your laughter echoing through the trees? For many of us, these memories serve as the foundation of our relationship with nature, shaping our perceptions and attitudes toward the world around us.

As we delve into the recesses of our minds to retrieve those formative outdoor experiences, we begin to unravel the intricate tapestry of emotions woven into each moment. Picture yourself standing at the foot of towering mountains, feeling a sense of awe that seems to stretch beyond the horizon. The grandeur of nature's majesty fills you with a humbling sense of wonder, reminding you of your place in the vastness of the universe.

Or perhaps you find yourself wandering through a sun-dappled forest, where every leaf and branch seems to dance in harmony with the gentle breeze. The rustle of leaves is underfoot and the chorus of birdsong overhead envelops you in a comforting embrace, as if the forest itself is whispering secrets of ancient wisdom just for you.

In these moments of connection, we discover a profound sense of belonging, as if we are an integral part of something far greater than ourselves. It's as if the very essence of nature reaches out to touch our souls, inviting us to join in its timeless dance of life and renewal. Each experience becomes a thread in the fabric of our being, weaving together memories that shape our understanding of the world and our place within it.

But our connection with nature extends far beyond our individual experiences; it is a bond that unites us all as members of the global community. In sharing our stories and listening to the experiences of others, we gain a deeper understanding of the diverse ways in which people connect with the natural world.

Imagine yourself nestled amongst friends, old and new, encircling a crackling campfire deep in the heart of the wilderness. The dancing flames cast a warm glow, illuminating the faces of those gathered as they eagerly shared their most cherished outdoor memories. Each tale unfolds like a chapter in a grand adventure book, transporting listeners to distant mountaintops, tranquil forests, and serene lakeshores.

One storyteller recalls the exhilarating rush of summiting a towering peak, their breath stolen away by the panoramic vista spread out below. They vividly describe the sensation of standing atop the world, the crisp mountain air tingling against their skin as they drink in the awe-inspiring beauty of nature's handiwork.

Another reminisces about the simple yet profound joy of witnessing a sunset transform the sky into a canvas of vibrant hues. They paint a picture with words, capturing the serene tranquility of the moment as the sun dips below the horizon, casting a golden glow across the landscape.

As each narrative unfolds, a sense of camaraderie fills the air, weaving a tapestry of shared experiences that transcend cultural boundaries and language barriers. The storytellers' voices mingle with the crackle of the fire and the chorus of nocturnal creatures, creating a symphony of connection that reverberates through the wilderness.

In these shared moments, we come to recognize the common threads that bind us together—the sense of wonder that accompanies witnessing a breathtaking natural phenomenon, the feeling of peace that settles over us when we immerse ourselves in the beauty of the wilderness. Amidst the flickering flames and star-studded skies, we find solace and solidarity, knowing that we are not alone in our love for the great outdoors.

As the night sky unfurls above us, a celestial canvas adorned with a multitude of twinkling stars, we are enveloped in a sense of awe and wonder, reminded of the values and passions that unite us in our quest for adventure. Whether it's a shared commitment to conservation and environmental stewardship or a mutual desire to seek out new experiences and push the boundaries of our comfort zones, our connection with nature is deeply rooted in a common purpose.

Consider the tale of a tight-knit group of friends whose bond is forged by their unwavering love for the great outdoors. United by a shared spirit of adventure, they come together to embark on an epic journey of exploration and discovery. Their expedition leads them through rugged mountain ranges, dense forests, and untamed wilderness, each step revealing new challenges and triumphs waiting to be conquered.

In the face of adversity, their camaraderie becomes their greatest strength. When fierce storms threaten to derail their progress, they huddle together under makeshift shelters, sharing stories and laughter to lift each other's spirits. When fatigue sets in and doubts creep into their minds, they draw inspiration from the collective determination of their group, finding renewed vigor to press onward.

Their journey is not without its moments of peril. They navigate treacherous terrain, scaling sheer cliffs and forging across rushing rivers with steely determination and unwavering resolve. Yet, with each obstacle overcome, they emerge stronger and more united than before, their shared experiences binding them together like the roots of ancient trees intertwined beneath the forest floor.

Through it all, their shared values serve as a guiding light, illuminating their path through the darkest of times. Their reverence for the natural world fuels their determination to protect and preserve it for future generations, inspiring them to tread lightly upon the land and leave only footprints behind.

As they gaze up at the star-strewn sky above, they are reminded of the vastness of the universe and their place within it. Bound by a common purpose and fueled by a shared passion for adventure, they stand together as a testament to the enduring power of friendship and the unbreakable bond between humanity and the natural world.

But perhaps the most inspiring stories are those of individuals who have found purpose and connection through their relationship with nature. From the conservationists working tirelessly to protect endangered species to the adventurer who braves the elements in search of new horizons, these individuals serve as beacons of hope and inspiration, reminding us of the transformative power of the natural world.

Consider the tale of Sherlitha Caldwell, a wife, mother, and former nurse, who understands this truth intimately. Behind the lens lies her journey—a tale of transformation ignited by personal tragedy and fueled by an unwavering passion for capturing life's fleeting moments.

In June of 2013, Caldwell's world was shaken by the passing of her beloved grandmother. As a dedicated nurse, the weight of her responsibilities coupled with the grief of loss took a toll on her health. The stress manifested physically, leading to panic attacks that left her feeling overwhelmed and adrift.

Driving one day, consumed by the demands of her job, Caldwell experienced a frightening numbness in her left side—a sensation she feared to be a stroke. Rushing herself to the hospital, she was relieved to find it was a panic attack instead. But this incident was a wake-up call, signaling the need for a profound change in her life.

Reluctantly, Caldwell found herself at a crossroads, grappling with the weight of her unrelenting panic attacks. Despite her initial hesitations, she bravely sought solace in the guidance of a psychologist—a decision not easily made, especially within communities of color where seeking mental health support can carry stigma.

Through the therapeutic journey that followed, Caldwell embarked on a profound exploration of her innermost struggles, ultimately unearthing the deeply buried grief stemming from her grandmother's passing. It was within the safe confines of therapy sessions that Caldwell encountered a pivotal moment of revelation, encapsulated in a deceptively simple yet remarkably transformative piece of advice: "Just take pictures."

With this newfound mantra echoing in her mind, Caldwell embarked on a profound odyssey that would redefine the trajectory of her life. Initially establishing herself as a Southern Soul Artist Photographer, she skillfully captured the soul-stirring essence of renowned musicians such as J1, Avail Hollywood, and T.K. Soul. Yet, as fate would have it, her journey took an unexpected turn when she ventured into the captivating realm of trail-riding photography.

In 2014, Caldwell boldly stepped into the vibrant tapestry of the trail riding scene, encountering initial skepticism and formidable challenges in earning the trust of its close-knit community. Undeterred by these obstacles, she distinguished herself through unwavering dedication, painstakingly immortalizing every fleeting moment—from the graceful riders to the breathtaking landscapes—with equal fervor and reverence. In doing so, Caldwell not only captured images but also hearts, cementing her place as an indispensable fixture within the trail-riding community.

As the years unfolded, Caldwell's steadfast commitment to her craft bore abundant fruit. By 2018, her photography endeavors had blossomed into a thriving source of income, surpassing the earnings from her esteemed nursing career. Fueled by this tangible manifestation of her passion, Caldwell found herself at a pivotal juncture, standing on the precipice of a life-altering decision.

In 2019, after two decades of dedicated service in the nursing profession, Caldwell made the courageous choice to bid farewell to the familiar confines of her career and wholeheartedly embrace the boundless possibilities of photography.

This transition not only marked a turning point in Caldwell's career but also ignited her passion for mentoring and music management. Drawing from her tumultuous upbringing, Caldwell now mentors young girls who, like her, lacked stable parental figures. Additionally, she manages a local Southern Soul artist named Hisyde, a role she embraces with pride and dedication.

Through it all, Caldwell remains grounded in her belief that her purpose is to uplift and support others. She has established her own studio and community group, lovingly referred to as the Gorilla Squad, comprising photographers, DJs, and small businesses. For Caldwell, photography is more than just capturing moments—it's a tool for empowerment and connection, a means of sharing stories and inspiring others to embrace their journeys.

As the shutter clicks and the images come to life, Sherlitha Caldwell's story serves as a reminder of the transformative power of passion, resilience, and the unwavering belief in one's potential. In the lens of Captured Moments by Sherlitha, every moment is precious, every story is significant, and every individual has the power to shape their narrative.

Chapter 4
Embracing the Adventure Ahead

As we embark on our outdoor journey together, setting the stage for an unforgettable adventure is essential. In this chapter, we will delve into the anticipation, preparation, and camaraderie that define the essence of our outdoor experience. From packing essentials to building group cohesion, let's embrace the adventure ahead with enthusiasm and excitement.

Anticipating the Journey Together:

The anticipation of an upcoming outdoor adventure is akin to a bubbling cauldron of excitement, curiosity, and endless possibility. It's a time when our senses are heightened, and our imaginations run wild with the promise of new experiences and unforgettable memories. As we eagerly await the journey ahead, let's delve deeper into the psychology behind this anticipation and explore the factors that contribute to its exhilarating nature.

Think back to a time when you embarked on an outdoor adventure—a moment frozen in time, brimming with anticipation and anticipation. Perhaps it was a challenging hike through rugged terrain, where every step brought you closer to the summit and the breathtaking vistas that awaited. Or maybe it was a serene camping trip under the canopy of stars, where the crackling of the campfire and the gentle rustle of the wind lulled you into a state of tranquil anticipation. Alternatively, it could have been a pulse-pounding whitewater rafting expedition, where the thrill of the rapids and the adrenaline rush of each twist and turn left you breathless with anticipation.

In the days leading up to your adventure, what emotions coursed through your veins? Was it a heady mixture of excitement and nervousness as you contemplated the challenges and triumphs that lay ahead? Or perhaps it was a sense of wonder and awe as you marveled at the unknown landscapes and untamed wilderness that awaited your exploration?

Sharing stories of past adventures is more than just a way to pass the time—it's a ritual that stirs the soul and ignites the flames of anticipation for the journey ahead. As we gather around the campfire or linger over a steaming cup of coffee, let's weave tales of triumph and tribulation, laughter and camaraderie, moments that tested our resolve, and moments that took our breath away. These stories serve not only to entertain but also to inspire and motivate us, reminding us of the indomitable spirit of adventure that lies within each of us.

In recounting our past adventures, we are transported back in time to moments of pure exhilaration and unbridled joy. We relive the challenges and obstacles we've conquered, drawing strength and courage from the memories that have shaped us into the adventurers we are today. And as we look ahead to the journey that lies before us, we do so with a renewed sense of purpose and determination, knowing that each step we take brings us closer to the thrill of the unknown and the promise of new discoveries.

Packing Essentials and Collaborating:

Effective preparation is the cornerstone of a successful outdoor adventure, laying the foundation for a safe and enjoyable experience amidst the wonders of nature. As we embark on our journey, let's delve into the intricacies of preparation, ensuring we have all the essentials to navigate the wilderness with confidence and ease.

Collaboration is the bedrock of efficient packing for any outdoor excursion. By harnessing the collective expertise and resources of our group, we can streamline the packing process and ensure that no essential item is overlooked. Assigning tasks such as meal planning, gear maintenance, and navigation allows each member to contribute their unique skills and insights, fostering a sense of camaraderie and teamwork from the outset.

Look Who's Outdoor

When assembling our gear and provisions, it's essential to prioritize the essentials that will sustain us throughout our adventure. Let's explore these key elements in detail:

1. **Shelter**: A sturdy tent or shelter serves as our sanctuary amidst the elements, providing refuge and respite after a day of exploration. Ensure that your shelter is durable, weather-resistant, and properly ventilated for maximum comfort and protection.
2. **Clothing**: Dressing in layers is essential for regulating body temperature and adapting to fluctuating weather conditions. Pack moisture-wicking base layers, insulating mid-layers, and waterproof outer layers to stay warm and dry in any environment.
3. **Food and Water**: Pack lightweight, nutrient-rich meals and ample hydration to sustain energy levels and replenish fluids throughout our journey. Consider options such as dehydrated meals, energy bars, and portable water filtration systems to optimize space and convenience.
4. **Navigation Tools**: Navigating unfamiliar terrain requires reliable navigation tools such as maps, compasses, or GPS devices. Familiarize yourself with our route and have backup navigation methods in place to ensure we stay on course and reach our destination safely.
5. **First Aid Kit**: Be prepared for minor injuries and medical emergencies with a comprehensive first aid kit containing essentials such as bandages, antiseptic wipes, pain relievers, and emergency medication. Regularly inspect and replenish your kit to ensure it remains fully stocked and up-to-date.
6. **Emergency Supplies**: In unforeseen circumstances, having emergency supplies on hand can be a lifesaver. Pack essential items such as a whistle, flashlight, emergency blanket, and multi-tool to address unexpected challenges and emergencies with confidence and resourcefulness.
7. **Personal Items**: Don't overlook the importance of personal hygiene and protection in the great outdoors. Pack essentials

such as sunscreen, insect repellent, lip balm, and toiletries to maintain comfort and wellness throughout our adventure.

By meticulously preparing and packing these essentials, we equip ourselves with the tools and resources needed to embark on our outdoor journey with confidence and resilience. Let's embrace the spirit of collaboration and preparation as we set forth into the wilderness, ready to explore, discover, and experience the wonders that await us.

Building Group Cohesion:

A cohesive group is essential for a successful outdoor adventure. By fostering unity and camaraderie, we can overcome challenges together and create lasting memories. Building group cohesion begins long before we set foot on the trail—it starts with open communication, mutual respect, and a shared sense of purpose.

One way to build group cohesion is through team-building activities and group exercises. Whether it's a trust fall, a ropes course, or a cooperative game, these activities encourage collaboration, communication, and trust among group members. By working together to overcome challenges, we strengthen our bonds and build a sense of solidarity.

Another important aspect of building group cohesion is establishing clear roles and responsibilities within the group. By assigning tasks based on individual strengths and skills, we can ensure that everyone feels valued and contributes to the success of the adventure. Whether it's leading the way on a hike, cooking a meal over the campfire, or tending to the needs of fellow adventurers, each member plays a vital role in the group dynamic.

A Reflection

In the spirit of personal reflection, let's dive into the remarkable story of Darius James, a man whose passion for the outdoors transcends the football fields of Texas and has led him to a purpose higher than the game itself.

Look Who's Outdoor

Growing up in the heart of Texas, where football is more than just a sport but a way of life, Darius found himself drawn to the gridiron like so many of his peers. With dreams of playing under the Friday night lights and earning a spot at the next level, Darius pursued his athletic career with determination and grit. However, amidst the crowd's roar and the thrill of competition, something else was always calling out to him—a quiet voice beckoning him to the serenity of the outdoors.

While his teammates were honing their skills on the field, Darius often sneaked away to local creeks and rivers drawn by the allure of fishing. It was here, surrounded by the peaceful rhythm of nature, that he felt most alive. Despite the disapproval of his coaches, Darius couldn't resist the pull of the water and the thrill of the chase.

As Darius matured, so too did his love for the outdoors. It wasn't long before his passion led him to his wife and ultimately to a purpose higher than football. Recognizing the importance of outdoor skills in today's world, particularly in the face of challenges like the pandemic and natural disasters, Darius founded Fillin' Freezers Outdoors—a nonprofit organization dedicated to teaching people of color the essential skills of fishing and hunting.

For Darius, fishing isn't just a hobby—it's a way of life. Whether he's casting his line in the waters of Kansas, North Carolina, Georgia, or his native Texas, Darius approaches each adventure with a sense of reverence and appreciation. His secret to success? Understanding the needs and desires of the fish and crafting his bait accordingly. From homemade concoctions of liver and stink bait to premade delights like chicken oil and strawberry Kool-Aid, Darius knows just what it takes to reel in the big catch.

But for Darius, the true joy of fishing lies not in the size of the catch but in the opportunity to share his love of the outdoors with his family. Whether he's teaching his children how to bait a hook or showing his wife the finer points of casting, Darius finds fulfillment in passing on his knowledge and passion to the next generation.

When asked what the outdoors means to him, Darius sums it up in three simple words: appreciation, dedication, and love. For him, the great outdoors isn't just a playground—it's a classroom, a sanctuary, and a source of endless wonder. Through Fillin' Freezers Outdoors, Darius is on a mission to ensure that everyone, regardless of background or circumstance, has the opportunity to experience the magic of nature and the thrill of the chase.

In reflecting on Darius' journey, we are reminded of the power of passion, purpose, and perseverance. His story serves as a testament to the transformative power of the outdoors and its profound impact on our lives. So, as we prepare to embark on our own outdoor adventure, let's take a page from Darius' book and approach each moment with appreciation, dedication, and love.

Chapter 5
Week 1 - Cycling Harmony

In the previous chapters, we've embarked on journeys of discovery, camaraderie, and personal growth in the great outdoors. Now, we're gearing up for a new adventure that brings us closer to nature, tests our limits, and ignites our sense of exploration: cycling.

Cycling is more than just a means of transportation; it's a lifestyle, a sport, and a gateway to unforgettable experiences. Whether you're a seasoned cyclist or a novice rider, there's something exhilarating about the feeling of freedom that comes from pedaling through scenic landscapes, feeling the wind in your hair, and the sun on your face.

The Thrill of Two Wheels

Picture this: as you pedal through rugged mountain trails, each turn of the wheel reveals new challenges and breathtaking vistas. The adrenaline rush of conquering steep inclines and navigating technical descents adds an element of thrill to the journey, making every ride an adventure in itself.

But it's not just the mountain trails that beckon cyclists; serene countryside roads offer a different kind of allure. Here, the rhythm of your pedals sets the pace as you glide through picturesque landscapes, with rolling hills and lush greenery stretching out as far as the eye can see. It's a sensory experience unlike any other, with nature's sights, sounds, and scents enveloping you in a cocoon of tranquility.

What sets cycling apart from other outdoor activities is its accessibility. With nothing more than a bike and a helmet, you have the freedom to explore almost anywhere your heart desires. The possibilities are endless, from bustling urban bike paths to remote wilderness trails. And the best part? Cycling is a low-impact exercise that's gentle on the joints, making it suitable for people of all ages and fitness levels.

But beyond its physical benefits, cycling also offers a mental and emotional escape from the stresses of everyday life. There's something liberating about the feeling of wind in your hair, the rhythmic cadence of your pedals, and the sense of freedom that comes from charting your own course. It's a form of meditation on wheels, allowing you to clear your mind, focus on the present moment, and connect with the world around you in a profound way.

Cycling is more than just a recreational activity; it's a journey of self-discovery, a celebration of the natural world, and a testament to the human spirit. So whether you're a seasoned cyclist or a novice rider, grab your bike, don your helmet, and embark on an adventure that will awaken your senses, rejuvenate your soul, and leave you craving for more.

Gear Up for Adventure

Before you embark on your cycling adventure, it's crucial to ensure you have the right gear and equipment to keep you safe, comfortable, and prepared for whatever the road or trail may throw your way. Here's a comprehensive guide to gearing up for cycling success:

1. **Choosing the Right Bike:** Your choice of bike will largely depend on the type of terrain you plan to tackle and your personal preferences. For speed and efficiency on smooth roads, a sleek road bike with narrow tires and a lightweight frame may be ideal. On the other hand, if you're venturing off-road or tackling rugged trails, a sturdy mountain bike with wider tires and durable suspension will provide the stability and control you need. Take the time to research and test-ride different bikes to find the perfect fit for your cycling style and goals.
2. **Protective Gear:** The most important piece of protective gear for any cyclist is a properly fitting helmet designed specifically for cycling. A helmet serves as your first line of defense in the

event of a fall or collision, reducing the risk of head injury and protecting your most vital asset—your brain. Look for a helmet that meets safety standards and provides a snug, comfortable fit.

3. **Apparel and Clothing:** Dressing appropriately for your cycling adventure is essential for staying comfortable and safe on the road or trail. Choose moisture-wicking clothing that will keep you dry and comfortable, even during intense rides. Opt for lightweight, breathable fabrics that offer flexibility and freedom of movement. Consider investing in padded cycling shorts for added comfort on long rides, and don't forget to layer up or down depending on the weather conditions.

4. **Repair and Maintenance Kit:** No cyclist should venture out without a basic repair and maintenance kit to handle on-the-go repairs and emergencies. Essential items to include in your kit are a tire pump or CO_2 inflator, tire levers for removing and replacing tires, a patch kit for repairing punctures, and a multi-tool with various wrenches, screwdrivers, and other tools for making adjustments and repairs to your bike. Additionally, carry spare tubes and a small supply of chain lubricant to keep your bike running smoothly.

5. **Hydration and Nutrition:** Staying fueled and hydrated is crucial for maintaining energy levels and performance during long rides. Carry a water bottle or hydration pack filled with plenty of fluids to stay hydrated throughout your ride, especially in hot or humid conditions. Pack nutrient-dense snacks such as energy bars, trail mix, or fresh fruit to replenish electrolytes and keep hunger at bay. Remember to refuel regularly to avoid hitting the dreaded "bonk" and ensure a satisfying and enjoyable cycling experience.

By equipping yourself with the right gear and taking the necessary precautions, you'll be well-prepared to tackle any cycling adventure with confidence and peace of mind. So gear up, hit the road or trail, and embark on a journey of exploration, discovery, and adventure on two wheels.

Exploring New Horizons

Once you're equipped with the right gear, it's time to hit the road—or trail—and embark on your cycling adventure. Like hiking, cycling offers a myriad of opportunities for exploration and discovery. Whether you're pedaling through a bustling cityscape or meandering along a tranquil forest path, each ride presents new sights, sounds, and experiences to savor.

One of the joys of cycling is the sense of freedom it provides. With the wind in your hair and the open road ahead, you're free to set your own pace, chart your own course, and explore to your heart's content. Cycling allows you to cover more ground than hiking, making it possible to visit multiple destinations in a single outing and discover hidden gems along the way.

Challenges and Triumphs

Like any adventure, cycling is not without its challenges. From steep climbs to technical descents, every ride presents obstacles to overcome and opportunities for growth. But it's in facing these challenges head-on, we discover our true strength and resilience.

Whether it's conquering a daunting hill climb or navigating a tricky descent, cycling pushes us out of our comfort zones and tests our limits in ways we never thought possible. But with perseverance, determination, and the support of our fellow riders, we can overcome any obstacle and emerge stronger on the other side.

Embracing the Journey

As we pedal our way through the ups and downs of our cycling adventure, it's important to pause and appreciate the journey itself. Cycling is not just about reaching the destination; it's about the experiences we gather along the way, the friendships we forge, and the memories we create.

So, take a moment to savor the sights and sounds of the road, to feel the rhythm of your heartbeat and the steady cadence of your pedals. Embrace the sense of freedom and possibility that comes from exploring the world on two wheels, and let the beauty of nature inspire and rejuvenate your spirit.

Justin Deshone: The Student's Champion

Reflecting on the journey of Justin Deshone through the streets of South Dallas, one cannot help but marvel at his profound impact on the community. A true Dallas native, Justin's connection to this neighborhood runs deep, stemming from his childhood experiences of play and camaraderie on these very streets.

As a dedicated educator and community advocate, Justin's commitment to the betterment of South Dallas goes beyond his role in the classroom or on the basketball court. At JJ Rhodes Elementary, where he is affectionately known as Coach J or THE STUDENTS' CHAMPION, Justin has become a beacon of hope and opportunity for the youth in a community often plagued by poverty and crime.

Over the years, Justin's efforts to uplift and empower the youth of South Dallas have been nothing short of inspiring. From organizing Christmas toy drives to leading community bike rides, he has consistently sought to provide moments of joy and normalcy in the lives of children who face adversity on a daily basis.

The recent bike ride through the streets of South Dallas was a testament to Justin's unwavering dedication and passion for his community. Originally planned for 2021, Justin felt compelled to organize the event sooner, recognizing the need to bring a sense of peace and positivity to a neighborhood grappling with challenges exacerbated by the pandemic.

What inspired Justin to spearhead the Bike Ride for the South Dallas youth and community was a desire to provide a sense of normalcy in a time of uncertainty. With COVID-19 restrictions limiting social interactions, Justin saw cycling as an opportunity for students to safely engage with their peers and families while enjoying the outdoors.

As the holiday season approaches, Justin shows no signs of slowing down in his mission to uplift the South Dallas community. With plans for a drive-thru Toy Giveaway featuring hundreds of brand-new toys, Justin continues to embody the spirit of service and compassion that defines his character.

In Justin Deshone, South Dallas has found a champion—a tireless advocate who leads by example, inspires others to act, and demonstrates love and generosity's transformative power. As we look to the future, let us draw inspiration from Justin's remarkable journey and work together to build a brighter, more resilient community for generations to come.

Chapter 6
Week 2 – Waterside Adventures

Waterside adventures have a magnetic allure, drawing us towards the vast expanse of lakes, rivers, and oceans, beckoning us to explore their mysteries and embrace their challenges. In this chapter, we dive headfirst into the realm of aquatic excursions, where every splash brings a new story of trust, preparation, triumph, and connection. Join us as we embark on a journey of discovery, navigating the waters with courage, camaraderie, and an insatiable thirst for adventure.

Introduction to Water Adventures

The gentle lapping of waves against the shore sets the stage for our aquatic odyssey. It's a realm where thrill-seekers find solace, and nature lovers discover the true meaning of freedom. Picture yourself gliding effortlessly across the glassy surface of a tranquil lake, the sun painting a masterpiece of light and shadow on the water's canvas. Or imagine the adrenaline rush as you navigate turbulent rapids, your paddle slicing through the frothy whitewater with precision and grace. Water adventures offer a symphony of sensations, from the soothing embrace of cool currents to the heart-pounding excitement of conquering mighty waves. But beyond the thrill lies a deeper connection – a bond forged between adventurers who share the same quest for exploration and discovery. It's a realm where trust reigns supreme, where every stroke of the oar and every breath beneath the surface is a testament to our unity with the elements.

The world of aquatic adventures is a mesmerizing realm where nature's elements converge to create unforgettable experiences. Did you know that lakes, rivers, and oceans cover over 70% of the Earth's surface? With such vast expanses of water to explore, there's no shortage of opportunities for thrill-seekers and nature enthusiasts alike to embark on their own aquatic odyssey.

Imagine yourself gliding effortlessly across the glassy surface of a tranquil lake at sunrise, surrounded by the serene beauty of nature awakening to a new day. Lakes, often formed by glaciers or tectonic activity, provide havens of tranquility where paddlers can escape the hustle and bustle of everyday life and connect with the rhythms of the natural world.

For those seeking an adrenaline rush, navigating turbulent rapids offers an exhilarating challenge. Did you know that whitewater rafting originated thousands of years ago, with indigenous peoples using primitive rafts to navigate rivers for trade, transportation, and exploration? Today, modern adventurers continue this tradition, harnessing the power of whitewater to test their skills and push their limits.

Water adventures offer a symphony of sensations, from the soothing embrace of cool currents to the heart-pounding excitement of conquering mighty waves. Did you know that the world's oceans contain an estimated 321 million cubic miles of water? Within this vast expanse lie untold treasures waiting to be discovered, from colorful coral reefs teeming with marine life to mysterious underwater caves shrouded in darkness.

But beyond the thrill of adventure, there lies a deeper connection that binds us together as explorers of the aquatic realm. It's a bond forged through shared experiences and mutual respect for the power of nature. Whether navigating rapids or paddling through calm waters, every stroke of the oar is a reminder of our unity with the elements and our shared quest for exploration and discovery.

So, whether you're a seasoned adventurer or a curious novice, the world of aquatic adventures beckons with endless possibilities. Embrace the thrill of the unknown, and let the gentle lapping of waves guide you on your own journey of exploration and discovery.

Preparing for Aquatic Excursions

Before embarking on our aquatic adventures, it's vital to prioritize safety and thorough preparation. Much like seasoned sailors plotting their course through unknown territories, we must arm ourselves with the essential knowledge and equipment to navigate the potential challenges that lie ahead.

Communication emerges as our most valuable asset, serving as the lifeline that ensures every member of our expedition is synchronized and prepared to confront whatever obstacles the elements may present.

Did you know that mastering the art of paddling isn't just about physical strength but also about technique and efficiency? Learning how to paddle effectively propels us forward and conserves energy for the journey ahead. It's a skill honed through practice and patience, with each stroke bringing us closer to mastering the rhythm of the water.

Furthermore, familiarizing ourselves with emergency procedures is crucial for safeguarding our well-being on the water. From understanding how to properly use safety equipment to know how to respond in unforeseen circumstances like capsizing or encountering wildlife, preparation can mean the difference between a minor setback and a major crisis.

Yet, beyond the practical aspects of preparation lies a profound lesson in trust and camaraderie. As we gather to share stories of past adventures and swap tips for navigating treacherous waters, bonds that extend far beyond mere companionship are forged. In these moments of shared vulnerability and mutual support, our team's true strength emerges, uniting us in our common pursuit of adventure and exploration.

By prioritizing safety, preparation, and the cultivation of trust, we lay the foundation for a successful and fulfilling aquatic excursion. With each paddle stroke and each shared laugh, we not only navigate the waters before us but also embark on a journey of personal growth and collective discovery.

Challenges and Triumphs

No adventure is without its trials and tribulations, and our journey on the water is no exception. As we embark upon our voyage, we find ourselves confronted by the unpredictable forces of nature, from sudden storms that lash at our vessel to treacherous currents that threaten to pull us off course. These formidable challenges serve as the crucible in which our mettle is tested, pushing us beyond our comfort zones and forcing us to confront our deepest fears.

Yet, precisely in these moments of adversity, the true essence of teamwork reveals itself. Bound by a shared purpose and a common goal, we come together as a unified force, drawing strength from one another to navigate the turbulent waters ahead. Each member of our crew plays a crucial role in our collective endeavor, offering support and encouragement when the seas grow rough, and the horizon seems distant.

Every obstacle we encounter reminds us of the indomitable spirit that resides within each of us. It is a spirit forged in the crucible of challenge and adversity, honed through perseverance and unwavering determination. And though the path ahead may be fraught with peril, we press on undaunted, guided by the unwavering belief that no obstacle is insurmountable and no goal beyond our reach.

As we confront each new challenge that lies before us, we do so with a sense of purpose and resolve, for we know that with every trial overcome comes a sense of triumph – a feeling of exhilaration that can only be achieved through perseverance and resilience. Whether it's successfully navigating a daunting rapid or weathering the fury of a sudden squall, every victory serves as a testament to the strength of our bond and the unyielding power of the human spirit.

And so, we press onward, buoyed by the knowledge that no matter what challenges may lie ahead, we will face them together as a team. For it is through adversity that true camaraderie is forged, and it is through perseverance that our greatest triumphs are achieved. And when, at last, we emerge victorious on the other side, we will do so not as individuals but as a united force – stronger, wiser, and more resilient than ever before.

Embracing Group Bonding Moments

Amidst the excitement of our adventures on the water, there are quiet moments that knit us together as a group. Imagine sitting around a crackling campfire, surrounded by the vastness of a starry sky. We share stories and jokes, feeling the warmth of camaraderie deep in our bones.

During the day, we explore hidden coves, their waters shimmering in shades of blue and green. We laugh as we dive in, feeling the cool embrace of the sea. These simple joys create bonds that last a lifetime.

Our shared experiences form a tapestry of memories. We remember the rush of adrenaline as we conquered challenging rapids and the peaceful beauty of sunsets reflecting off the water's surface. These moments remind us of the power of friendship and human connection.

As we journey together, we find strength in each other's company. Every obstacle we face becomes a shared triumph, and every memory becomes a treasure to hold close to.

Chevaughn Dixon: Paddling Towards Equity and Adventure

In the vast expanse of outdoor adventures, there are individuals who not only embrace the thrill of exploration but also strive to make these experiences accessible to all. One such pioneer is Chevaughn Dixon, a trailblazer in the world of kayaking and a champion for diversity and inclusion in outdoor sports.

Chevaughn's journey into the world of kayaking began with a simple curiosity – a desire to explore something beyond the traditional realm of sports like basketball and soccer. A chance encounter with the river sparked his interest, leading him down a path that would redefine his understanding of adventure and community.

What drew Chevaughn to kayaking wasn't just the exhilaration of paddling through rushing waters; it was the opportunity to connect with people from all walks of life. Chevaughn found himself immersed in a diverse tapestry of individuals, each with a unique story to tell, from doctors to lawyers, engineers to environmental scientists.

But it wasn't long before Chevaughn's passion for kayaking evolved into something more profound – a commitment to providing equitable access to outdoor adventures for underserved communities. Through his non-profit organization, Hudson River Riders, Chevaughn works tirelessly to break down barriers and empower black and brown youth to embrace the wonders of the natural world.

As one of the few black kayakers in a predominantly white sport, Chevaughn understands the challenges of being a trailblazer in uncharted waters. Yet, despite the obstacles he faces, he remains undeterred in his mission to create a more inclusive outdoor community.

For Chevaughn, the lack of diversity in kayaking isn't just a matter of representation; it's a question of equity and opportunity. With the high cost of equipment and training, many low-income individuals are effectively priced out of the sport, perpetuating cycles of exclusion and inequality.

But Chevaughn believes that kayaking isn't just a sport – it's a gateway to a world of possibilities. Beyond the thrill of adventure lies a wealth of knowledge waiting to be discovered, from marine biology to environmental science. Chevaughn hopes to inspire the next generation of environmental stewards and outdoor enthusiasts by providing access to outdoor activities.

Despite the challenges he faces as a black kayaker, Chevaughn remains steadfast in his commitment to creating a more inclusive outdoor community. Through his advocacy and outreach efforts, he strives to ensure that everyone, regardless of race or background, has the opportunity to experience the transformative power of outdoor adventure.

As Chevaughn paddles towards new horizons, he serves as a beacon of inspiration for adventurers everywhere, reminding us that the true spirit of exploration lies in conquering the unknown and building bridges of understanding and inclusion along the way.

Chapter 7
Week 3 – Climbing Together

Understanding Group Climbing

Climbing in a group, also known as multi-pitch or team climbing, offers an immersive and thrilling experience in the great outdoors. Unlike climbing solo, it's all about teamwork, communication, and achieving goals together. It's not just about the physical challenge; it's a true test of trust and camaraderie amidst nature's rough beauty.

Picture this: you're scaling rocky cliffs alongside your fellow climbers, each person playing a part in the adventure. It's like a dance, with everyone working together to secure ropes, find the best handholds, and support each other along the way. In this dynamic setting, it's not just about your skills but also about leaning on your teammates for support and motivation.

The heart of group climbing lies in the journey itself. As you gear up and prepare to ascend, there's a buzz of excitement in the air. With every move upward, you're not just conquering the rocks; you're forming bonds that go beyond the vertical landscape, sharing in the triumphs and challenges as one tight-knit unit.

Group climbing isn't just about physical strength; it's a testament to teamwork and resilience. As you navigate the cliffs, you're not just trusting your gear but also placing trust in your climbing buddies. Communication is key, with gestures and words guiding each climb and fostering a sense of unity among the heights.

Choosing Your Climbing Challenge

Embarking on a group climbing expedition is akin to setting sail on a thrilling odyssey, requiring meticulous planning and a keen eye for the perfect challenge. It's not merely about conquering the tallest or most imposing rock face; it entails thoughtful consideration of each team member's abilities, experience levels, and aspirations.

Selecting the optimal climbing route entails more than just a spontaneous decision at the foot of the cliff. It involves a collaborative process that kicks off with extensive deliberations among the team members. They pore over guidebooks, meticulously study maps, and dissect route descriptions, carefully evaluating factors such as difficulty, technical complexity, length, and potential hazards.

As they delve deeper into the intricacies of each potential route, climbers also contemplate the psychological and emotional hurdles that may lie ahead. Every voice within the group is valued, nurturing an atmosphere of inclusivity and mutual respect. Through candid dialogue, they gain a nuanced understanding of the challenges awaiting them, enabling them to make informed decisions.

Choosing a climbing challenge isn't solely about technical considerations; it's also about aligning with the collective aspirations and goals of the team. Whether their aim is to push personal boundaries, hone their skills, or revel in the exhilaration of exploration, each member's input helps shape the trajectory of the adventure.

Ultimately, the essence of the endeavor transcends mere summit attainment; it's about the journey itself. It's about embarking on an expedition as a cohesive unit, where the bonds forged through teamwork and encouragement are just as significant as the heights they aspire to reach. By selecting a route that resonates with the entire team, they ensure that every step forward becomes a shared triumph, and every obstacle surmounted fortifies their unity.

Supporting Each Other

In the realm of group climbing, support isn't just a fleeting gesture; it's the bedrock upon which every ascent is built. It encompasses a rich fabric of encouragement, guidance, and camaraderie, forming the cornerstone of every climber's journey. Here, teamwork reigns supreme, with climbers leaning on one another for safety, motivation, and emotional bolstering throughout their expedition.

Effective communication serves as the pivotal point of this dynamic, with climbers employing a diverse array of tools – be it gestures, uplifting words, or shared wisdom gleaned from past adventures – to solidify trust and solidarity among the team. Each interaction serves to reinforce the bonds that bind them together as they confront the vertical challenges that lie ahead.

Upon the rugged rock face, climbers orchestrate a symphony of support, leveraging their unique strengths to bolster the collective endeavor. Whether it's expertly belaying a partner or offering sage advice on technique, every action undertaken reflects a shared commitment and interdependence among the team members.

Yet, the essence of support extends beyond the physical realm, encompassing a deep reservoir of emotional reassurance and fortitude. In moments of fatigue or uncertainty, the team rallies together, providing solace and strength, knowing full well that they stand united in the face of adversity.

In the world of group climbing, inclusivity reigns supreme, ensuring that each member's voice is heard and valued. Through the cultivation of an environment steeped in trust and encouragement, climbers create a sanctuary wherein they can test their limits and unearth their true potential.

Ultimately, this collective sense of purpose and solidarity distinguishes group climbing. Through their steadfast support for one another, climbers forge bonds that transcend the mere act of climbing, uniting in a shared pursuit of adventure, challenge, and self-discovery.

Gaining New Perspectives

Embarking on the journey of climbing isn't merely about the physical act of scaling cliffs or overcoming external challenges; it's a profound voyage of self-discovery that unfolds amidst nature's awe-inspiring landscape. Each ascent serves as more than just a test of muscle; it's a deeply introspective journey that demands grit, focus, and resilience.

Look Who's Outdoor

Imagine this: as climbers ascend, they're not merely confronting the rugged terrain but also their own fears and limitations. Every challenging stretch and vertigo-inducing height becomes a reflective surface, revealing both their inner strength and vulnerabilities. With each step forward, they draw upon hidden reservoirs of courage, shattering self-imposed barriers and reshaping their perception of what they're capable of achieving.

However, climbing isn't solely a physical endeavor; it's also a spiritual odyssey. Amidst the breathtaking beauty of nature's wonders, climbers find solace in their souls. The rhythmic cadence of their breath and the symphony of wind and stone all contribute to moments of profound contemplation and connection with the natural world.

Perched on the edge of the cliff, climbers grapple with their inner demons, confronting doubts and insecurities head-on. And with every summit conquered, they emerge physically stronger and mentally fortified, armed with a newfound sense of confidence and empowerment to confront life's adversities.

Yet, the importance of climbing extends beyond mere conquest; it's about rediscovering our connection with the world around us. Standing atop a peak with sweeping panoramas stretching before them, climbers are humbled by the beauty and vastness of nature, serving as a poignant reminder of their place in the grand tapestry of existence.

Climbing isn't just a sport; it's a journey of self-discovery and growth. It's a testament to the resilience of the human spirit, a celebration of our ability to overcome obstacles and emerge stronger, wiser, and more attuned to the wonders of the world. Through climbing, we conquer mountains and ourselves, unlocking a deeper understanding of life's beauty and complexity along the way.

Personal Anecdotes

Personal tales aren't just stories in the exhilarating realm of climbing; they're vibrant threads weaving together a tapestry of shared adventure, revealing the magic of exploration and the bonds it creates. Among these narratives, two stand out as beacons of friendship, perseverance, and the undying spark of curiosity.

Step into the epic saga of Tommy Caldwell and Kevin Jorgeson as they embark on the monumental feat of conquering the Dawn Wall. This legendary rock face, nestled within the majestic expanse of El Capitan in Yosemite National Park, serves as the backdrop for their awe-inspiring journey, which captivated the hearts and minds of climbers around the globe.

Tommy and Kevin dedicated years of their lives to mastering the intricate sequences and daunting challenges presented by the Dawn Wall. With unwavering determination, they meticulously planned and trained, honing their skills to perfection in preparation for the monumental task ahead.

Despite facing numerous setbacks and encountering skeptics along the way, the bond of friendship between Tommy and Kevin remained steadfast. Throughout the highs and lows of their ascent, they leaned on each other for strength and encouragement and shared moments of laughter amidst the adversity.

Their journey transcended mere physical conquest; it symbolized the human spirit's resilience and camaraderie's power in the face of seemingly insurmountable odds. As they navigated the treacherous terrain of the Dawn Wall, their bond deepened, forging a connection that soared beyond the vertical realm.

Similarly, the adventure of Angela VanWiemeersch and Pamela Shanti Pack tackling Utah's Triple Crown resonates with echoes of friendship and triumph. Setting their sights on summiting three iconic desert towers—Castleton Tower, The Rectory, and The Priest—Angela and Pamela were drawn together by a love for exploration and a thirst for adventure. Despite their diverse backgrounds and skill levels, they tackled the challenge with a spirit of teamwork and camaraderie. Together, they navigated the intricate routes and sandstone spires, overcoming obstacles with grit and grace. With each peak conquered, their friendship blossomed, fueled by shared laughter, challenges, and a mutual adoration for the untamed wilderness they explored. Their journey speaks volumes about the transformative power of climbing, the bonds it forges, and the enduring allure of adventure that binds kindred souls.

These stories, alongside numerous others, provide captivating insights into the heart of climbing—a realm where enduring friendships are forged amidst the formidable challenges, exhilarating triumphs, and the majestic beauty of the natural world. Within these narratives lie a wellspring of inspiration, a sense of camaraderie, and the timeless realization that the most unforgettable adventures are those experienced alongside cherished souls who share in the journey's highs and lows.

Chapter 8
Week 4 - Thrill Seekers Unite

Introduction to Adrenaline Adventures

In the world of outdoor enthusiasts, there's a special kind of person – someone who craves excitement like it's their lifeline. These are the thrill-seekers, the daredevils who live for that heart-pounding rush of adrenaline that comes from pushing themselves to the limit. As we dive into Week 4 of our adventure challenge, we're celebrating these brave souls by diving headfirst into the thrilling world of adrenaline adventures.

Adrenaline adventures cover a wide range of activities, from the extreme heights of skydiving and BASE jumping to the intense challenges of whitewater rafting and rock climbing. What sets these activities apart is the element of danger – the thrill of facing your fears head-on and coming out on top. It's that spine-tingling feeling of knowing you've conquered something that once scared you silly.

In the world of adrenaline adventures, every jump, every rush of rapids, and every climb is like a bold declaration of human courage and curiosity. It's a place where normal rules don't apply, where the excitement of the unknown pulls us in like a magnet. For those brave enough to step into this electrifying world, each moment is like a thrilling song, showing off the unstoppable spirit of adventure within us.

Preparing for Extreme Experiences

Before diving headfirst into the thrilling world of adrenaline adventures, it's crucial to understand that safety comes first, no matter what. Unlike chill outdoor activities, where the main goal is just to relax and have fun, adrenaline adventures require serious preparation and attention to detail.

One of the most important parts of getting ready for these adventures is making sure we have the right gear and that it's in good shape. Our gear is like our lifeline out there – it's what keeps us safe when things get intense. From harnesses and ropes to helmets and protective gear, every single piece has to be double-checked to make sure it's working properly. Even the smallest mistake could have serious consequences, so it's super important to be really careful when inspecting and maintaining our gear.

Before setting off on any adventure, it's absolutely vital to carefully check all of our gear, even the smallest details. We have to go over our harnesses with a fine-tooth comb, making sure there are no signs of wear and tear that could make them less safe. These harnesses are what keep us secure when we're doing something intense, so they need to be in top shape. And when it comes to our ropes, which are like our lifelines, we have to be super thorough, looking for even the tiniest signs of damage. Because if they're compromised, it could lead to real trouble when we're out there facing challenges.

And let's not forget about our helmets – they're super important, too. Making sure our helmets fit just right is key, not only for comfort but also for keeping us safe from serious head injuries. We have to pay attention to the quality of materials, too, because if they're not up to scratch, they might not protect us as they should in case something goes wrong.

Making sure our gear is ready for adrenaline adventures isn't just important; it's crucial. It's all about keeping ourselves safe so we can really enjoy the thrill without worrying about getting hurt. By taking the time to check and maintain our gear regularly, we're reducing the chances of anything going wrong and increasing the chances of having an amazing time filled with excitement and triumph rather than danger and regret.

But being prepared isn't just about the physical stuff; it's also about getting our minds in the right place. It's totally normal to feel nervous before diving into something unknown and thrilling. But by mentally getting ourselves ready and imagining ourselves succeeding, we can build up the confidence we need to take on any challenge that comes our way.

Encouraging Each Other's Courage

The special bond that forms during adrenaline adventures is something truly powerful. In the midst of all the excitement and thrill, there's a connection that goes beyond just having fun together. It's like we become a family, sharing in these wild experiences and supporting each other through every twist and turn.

When things get risky and scary, there's this instinctual pull to stick together. We're all in it together, facing our fears and pushing ourselves to the limit. It's during these moments of uncertainty that the true meaning of camaraderie shines through. We come together, lifting each other up with words of encouragement and unwavering support.

In the world of adrenaline-fueled adventures, having a supportive team by your side is like having a lifeline. It's what keeps us going when things get tough, infusing every moment with a feeling of togetherness and purpose. Whether it's a simple word of encouragement before a nerve-wracking bungee jump or a comforting hand during the wild twists and turns of a whitewater rafting trip, knowing that you have fellow adventurers cheering you on makes all the difference.

When faced with scary challenges and big obstacles, having others on the journey with you gives you the courage to keep going. Each person in the group becomes a source of strength and inspiration, someone you can rely on when things get rough. And when we achieve something amazing together, it creates a bond that lasts a lifetime. These shared experiences become cherished memories, stitching us together in a tapestry of friendship and adventure that stays with us long after the rush of excitement has passed.

Treasuring Shared Moments of Thrill

As the thrill of adventure fades and we bid farewell to another unforgettable journey, it's the memories we've created together that leave the deepest imprint on our minds. Whether it's the rush of soaring through the sky or the sheer joy of conquering a towering peak, these shared moments forge a strong sense of camaraderie among us adventurers.

These instances of shared excitement remind us of the remarkable strength that comes from human connection. They're reminders of how powerful we can be when we face challenges together, united as one. These experiences tie us together, forming a narrative of resilience and triumph that transcends any limits of time or distance.

In the beautiful tapestry of life, the memories we've woven together through adventure and triumph stand out like precious gems. These shared experiences are more than just moments; they're treasures we hold dear, shining brightly as sources of inspiration and togetherness. They're the stories we'll eagerly share around campfires and dinner tables, each retelling strengthening the bonds of camaraderie and solidarity among us.

As we look back on these exhilarating moments of excitement and victory, we're reminded of the deep importance of human connection in our journey through life. These shared adventures remind us that no matter what challenges we face, we're never truly alone. In the embrace of friendship and solidarity, we find a strength that goes beyond what we can achieve alone. It's this unity that drives us forward with unwavering determination and resolve, ready to take on whatever lies ahead.

Personal Reflections

When we think back on all the exciting adventures we've had, it's clear that they've had a big impact on us. These experiences have taught us some important lessons. They've shown us how important it is to find courage when we're facing our fears, and they've reminded us how crucial it is to keep pushing forward, even when things get tough, as we chase our dreams.

Amidst all these moments of understanding and growth, what really stands out is how important our community is. When we come together with people who share our passions, it's like a spark igniting a fire. This shared energy propels us forward, helping us achieve things we never thought possible.

Being part of a community has taught us the power of working together. It's like we're all in this big team, pushing each other to reach new heights. And when we look ahead to the future, we do it with a sense of purpose, knowing that we're not alone. We're part of something bigger, something supportive.

Facing challenges becomes easier when we know we have a community behind us. Together, we can overcome anything that comes our way. It's through this collective effort that we discover our true potential and achieve success, time and time again.

Chapter 9
Reflecting on the Journey Together

As I huddle close to the flickering glow of the campfire, surrounded by the symphony of nature's nocturnal chorus, memories of our journey together come alive in the dancing shadows cast by the flames. It's been quite the ride, hasn't it? A journey fueled not only by my curiosity and desire for discovery but also by the bonds of friendship and camaraderie woven into the fabric of our adventure.

What truly sets this experience apart is the profound transformation undergone—both individually and within our group. In the moments of challenge and triumph, of laughter and introspection, I've found myself growing in ways I never imagined possible. Each obstacle overcome and shared victory celebrated has been a testament to the resilience and strength within.

But perhaps even more remarkable is the depth of connection forged along the way. Through shared experiences and struggles, bonds have been woven that transcend the boundaries of mere friendship, evolving into something deeper and more meaningful. In the quiet moments of conversation around the fire and the shared laughter under the starlit sky, the true richness of human connection is revealed.

As I sit here, surrounded by the warmth of the flames and the embrace of the wilderness, I'm reminded of just how far I've come. And as I gaze into the depths of the fire, gratitude fills me for the journey shared and the growth it has inspired within.

Celebrating Group Growth and Connections

The transformative power of adventure is undeniable. Studies have shown that engaging in outdoor activities together can lead to increased trust, improved communication, and strengthened bonds among group members. According to a study published in the Journal of Adventure Education and Outdoor Learning, shared outdoor experiences have been linked to heightened feelings of cohesion and cooperation within groups, making them an ideal setting for fostering personal and relational growth.

Our journey has been no exception. From the moment we set out into the wilderness, we were confronted with challenges that tested our physical abilities, resilience, and determination. Whether navigating rugged terrain, braving inclement weather, or overcoming our fears and limitations, each obstacle we faced served as an opportunity for growth and self-discovery.

But perhaps even more profound than our individual growth has been strengthening our collective bond. As we worked together to overcome obstacles and achieve our shared goals, we formed a sense of camaraderie that transcended mere friendship. We became a tight-knit community, united by a common purpose and a shared sense of adventure.

Expressing Gratitude and Appreciation

As we gather together beneath the vast expanse of the night sky, with the soft glow of the stars above us and the gentle rustle of leaves around us, this overwhelming feeling of gratitude is washing over us. It's like this warm, fuzzy sensation that wraps around our hearts, making us feel all cozy and content.

It's pretty neat how science has shown that when we take a moment to say "thanks" for the good stuff in our lives, it actually does something pretty cool to our brains. It makes us feel happier and more connected to the people around us. So, as we're sitting here, taking it all in, we're reminded of just how awesome it is to have each other.

Think about all those nights we've spent together, gathered around the crackling campfire, sharing stories and jokes. The laughter echoing through the darkness, the warmth of the fire against the chill of the night—it's these moments that stick with us, you know? They're like little snapshots of joy that we can look back on and smile about.

And then there are those times when we've just sat quietly together, soaking up the beauty of nature all around us. It's like being wrapped in a cozy blanket of peace and tranquility, with nothing but the sounds of the wilderness to keep us company. It's like time slows down in those moments, and we can appreciate the simple beauty of just being together.

Each memory we've made together feels like a precious gift, something to be cherished and treasured. Whether it's the big, epic adventures or the small, everyday moments, they all add up to make our lives more prosperous and more meaningful. So, as we sit here tonight, surrounded by the beauty of nature and the warmth of friendship, let's take a moment to say thanks—for all the laughs, all the quiet moments, and all the memories that make life so darn wonderful.

Setting Intentions for Future Adventures

As we peer into the velvety darkness that stretches before us, our thoughts naturally gravitate towards the exciting journeys that await. It's fascinating how research has uncovered the potency of setting intentions—it's like laying down tracks for a train, giving us a clear path to follow towards our goals. By visualizing the adventures on our horizon and plotting concrete objectives, we're giving ourselves a roadmap to success, fueling our drive with purpose and determination.

Our intentions are bold and ambitious. We aim to step outside our comfort zones, embracing challenges that will push us to our physical and mental limits. In these moments of growth and discomfort, we indeed come alive, expanding our capabilities and uncovering new layers of strength within ourselves.

But it's not just about conquering physical peaks; it's also about delving deeper into the heart of nature, forging a profound connection with the world around us. We yearn to explore unfamiliar landscapes, immerse ourselves in the raw beauty of untouched wilderness, and cultivate a reverence for the natural wonders surrounding us.

With each new adventure, we pledge to emerge more potent, more resilient, and more tightly knit as a team. It's in the shared triumphs and challenges that our bonds are strengthened, weaving a tapestry of camaraderie that binds us together in purpose and passion. So, as we set forth into the unknown, guided by the power of intention, we do so with hearts ablaze with excitement and minds primed for the extraordinary.

Expressing Love and Commitment

As the crackling flames of the fire gradually dim and the stillness of the night settles in around us, we turn to each other with an unmistakable warmth in our gazes, a silent acknowledgment of the love and commitment that binds us together. It's remarkable how research has illuminated the power of expressing affection and support within our group dynamics—like nourishing roots that intertwine to strengthen the tree of our unity.

In these tender moments, as we affirm our love and dedication to one another, we're fortifying the foundation upon which our relationships stand. In these gestures of care and affirmation, we weave threads of trust and understanding, fostering a sense of belonging and connection that runs deep within our collective spirit.

We make a solemn vow to stand by each other through all of life's twists and turns, to be each other's cheerleaders in moments of triumph and pillars of strength in times of adversity. Our commitment goes beyond mere friendship; it's a sacred pact forged through the crucible of shared experiences and mutual respect.

As we cast our gaze toward the horizon of the future, our hearts swell with an overwhelming sense of love and gratitude for the privilege of journeying together. The unwavering support of our companions buoys each step forward; each challenge met with the reassurance of knowing that we're not alone. And so, with hearts united and spirits ablaze, we embrace the adventures that lie ahead, secure in the knowledge that together, we can conquer anything.

Personal Reflections

Look Who's Outdoor

As the night gently embraces us and the embers of the fire fade into the darkness, we each take a moment to pause and reflect on the journey that has unfolded before us. With pen in hand and journal at the ready, we delve into the depths of our hearts and minds, eager to capture the essence of our shared adventure.

It's incredible how research has highlighted the transformative power of journaling—it's like a mirror that allows us to glimpse our innermost thoughts and emotions, guiding us on a journey of self-discovery and growth. As we put pen to paper, we open ourselves up to a world of introspection, where clarity and insight await.

We write of the challenges that tested our resolve and the lessons that emerged from adversity, each trial a stepping stone on the path to personal growth. We capture the laughter and camaraderie that filled our days, the bonds of friendship that were forged in the crucible of shared experiences. But beyond the surface, we delve deeper, exploring the profound impact this journey has had on each of us, individually and as a cohesive unit.

In the pages of our journals, we articulate the growth we've undergone, the barriers we've overcome, and the transformations that have taken root within us. We celebrate the connections that have blossomed, the moments of vulnerability that have deepened our bonds, and the unspoken language of love and gratitude that flows between us.

As we commit our final thoughts and feelings to paper, we are reminded of the power of reflection—the ability to pause, to ponder, and to glean wisdom from our experiences. As we close our journals and retire to our tents for the night, our hearts are filled with a profound sense of fulfillment, knowing that we have embarked on a journey of self-discovery and camaraderie that will stay with us long after the embers have faded and the stars have dimmed.

With a gentle sigh, we fold the pages of our journals and tuck them away, their inked reflections capturing the essence of our shared experiences. As we nestle into the warmth of our sleeping bags, a comforting sense of unity envelops us—the knowledge that we will have each other as steadfast companions amidst the uncertainties of tomorrow's adventures.

With this assurance in our hearts, we surrender to the embrace of slumber, lulled by the soft symphony of nature's nocturnal chorus. Beneath the celestial canopy, where stars twinkle like distant beacons of possibility, we drift into dreams tinged with the promise of new horizons and shared triumphs. And as the night enfolds us in its velvety embrace, we find solace in the bonds of camaraderie that transcend the darkness, guiding us toward the dawn of yet another day filled with anticipation and wonder.

Chapter 10
Continuing the Adventure Together

Welcome back, adventurers! Can you believe we've made it to the final chapter of our outdoor adventure journey together? It's been quite the ride, filled with challenges, triumphs, and unforgettable moments. From scaling the rugged cliffs to forging paths through dense rainforests, our expedition has been a testament to the human spirit's boundless thirst for exploration.

As we look ahead to new adventures, let's take some time to reflect on our journey so far and prepare ourselves for what lies ahead. Let's reminisce about the nights spent under a canopy of stars, sharing stories around crackling campfires and finding solace in the whispers of the wind through the trees. Let's remember the camaraderie forged in the face of adversity, the moments of awe as we beheld nature's grandeur in all its majesty.

But our journey doesn't end here; it merely evolves. As we bid farewell to familiar trails and landscapes, let's carry with us the lessons learned, the friendships forged, and the memories cherished. Let's heed the call of distant mountains, uncharted territories, and the siren song of the wild, for there is still so much left to explore and discover.

So, fellow adventurers, let's embark on this final leg of our odyssey with hearts full of gratitude, minds open to new experiences, and spirits as indomitable as the wilderness itself. Together, let's write the closing chapter of this epic saga, knowing that the greatest adventures are yet to come.

Looking Ahead to New Adventures

As we stand at the cliff of new beginnings, the air tingles with a profound sense of excitement and anticipation. The great outdoors beckons, its vast expanse stretching out before us like a canvas waiting to be painted with the brushstrokes of our adventures. There's always another peak to conquer, another trail to forge, another river to navigate, each offering a tempting glimpse into the mysteries of nature.

But beyond the physical challenges that await us, it's the intangible essence of adventure that truly ignites our spirits. Think back to those moments that stirred something deep within you, moments that now reside as cherished memories in the scrapbook of your mind. Perhaps it was the exhilarating rush of adrenaline coursing through your veins as you conquered a difficult climb, your heart pounding in rhythm with the pulse of the wilderness. Or maybe it was the overwhelming sense of awe that washed over you as you stood at the summit, witnessing a breathtaking scene that stretched to the horizon and beyond.

Whatever those moments may be, hold onto them tightly, for they are the fuel that will power you through the trials and triumphs of your future adventures. It's that insatiable thirst for exploration, that uncontainable sense of wonder and curiosity, that sets adventurers like us apart. So, as we stand on the threshold of new horizons, let us carry with us the echoes of past triumphs and the promise of future conquests, for the greatest adventures are yet to come.

Setting Group Goals

One of the most fulfilling aspects of boarding on adventures together is the shared pursuit of common goals. Whether you're navigating rugged trails with friends, loved ones, or fellow thrill-seekers, setting collective objectives serves as a catalyst for camaraderie and teamwork, enriching the journey with shared triumphs and collective memories.

Gather your adventure companions around the campfire or beneath the starlit sky and engage in a dialogue about your collective aspirations. Perhaps you aspire to conquer the summit of a towering peak, traverse a challenging multi-day trek, or master the art of wilderness survival. Whatever the ambition, ensure that it resonates with the spirit of your group and that it embodies the essence of adventure: daring, exhilarating, and, above all, enjoyable.

As we've journeyed together, we've encountered our fair share of obstacles and setbacks. Yet, through unwavering determination and the unwavering support of one another, we've emerged stronger and more resilient. Carry this lesson with you as you embark on new adventures with your companions, drawing inspiration and strength from each other's unwavering resolve.

Remember, the path ahead may be uptight and filled with challenges, but with unity, perseverance, and a shared sense of purpose, there's no peak too high, no trail too treacherous, and no goal too ambitious. Together, let's embrace the journey, celebrate the victories, and conquer the unknown, one adventure at a time.

Final Thoughts and Farewell

As our grand adventure together draws to a close, it's crucial to pause and reflect on the extraordinary voyage we've undertaken and the invaluable lessons we've gleaned along the way. From the dizzying heights of towering peaks to the tranquil serenity of hidden valleys, our journey has been a kaleidoscope of emotions, each moment leaving an indelible imprint on our hearts and souls.

Yet, as we prepare to turn the final page of this chapter, let us not mourn its conclusion but instead celebrate the myriad experiences that have enriched our lives. For in every challenge faced and every obstacle overcome, we have unearthed reservoirs of strength, resilience, and fortitude that we never knew existed within us.

As we stand on the brink of a new dawn, let us welcome the unknown with open arms, for it is the crucible in which our truest selves are forged. With every step into uncharted territory, we carry with us the wisdom and insights garnered from our shared journey, equipping us to navigate the twists and turns of fate with courage and conviction.

So, my fellow adventurers, as we bid adieu to this chapter of our lives, let us embrace the promise of new beginnings with unwavering optimism and boundless enthusiasm. For though the path ahead may be shrouded in uncertainty, we march forward unafraid, knowing that we are the architects of our destiny and that the greatest adventures are yet to unfold.

Personal Reflections

Before we bid our farewells and embark on our individual paths, I extend to you one final, heartfelt invitation: indulge in a moment of introspection. Find a secluded nook amidst the embrace of nature, armed with nothing but pen and parchment, and allow your thoughts to wander freely.

Reflect on the tapestry of experiences woven throughout our shared journey and the dreams that whisper softly within the recesses of your heart. What aspirations ignite the flames of passion within you? What lofty summits do you yearn to conquer, both metaphorically and literally? Take this opportunity to articulate your hopes, dreams, and aspirations for the future, for it is in the act of dreaming that we manifest our destinies.

Consider the invaluable lessons gleaned from our adventures together—lessons in resilience, determination, and the boundless capacity of the human spirit. How will you integrate these teachings into the fabric of your being, forging a path illuminated by the guiding light of wisdom?

Above all, ponder how you will carry the spirit of adventure with you as you traverse the uncharted territories that lie ahead. Let it be your steadfast companion, guiding you through the labyrinth of life's uncertainties with courage, curiosity, and an insatiable thirst for discovery.

As we bid adieu, know that our parting is but a fleeting moment in the grand tapestry of existence. Our paths may diverge, but the memories we've forged together shall forever linger, etched into the annals of time.

Farewell, dear companions, and may the winds of fortune carry you to realms beyond imagination. Until we reunite amidst the rustling leaves and winding trails, continue to explore, dream, and embrace the exhilarating journey that is life itself.

www.ingramcontent.com/pod-product-compliance
Lightning Source LLC
LaVergne TN
LVHW061602070526
838199LV00077B/7146